PICTURES IN PATCHWORK

Marie-Janine Solvit

Photographs from ELLE

STERLING
PUBLISHING CO., INC. NEW YORK

Oak Tree Press Co., Ltd.
London & Sydney

OTHER BOOKS OF INTEREST

Alkema's Scrap Magic
Appliqué and Reverse Appliqué
Bargello Stitchery
Beautiful Crafts Book
Creating from Remnants
Creative Lace-Making
Family Book of Crafts
Giant Book of Crafts

Hooked and Knotted Rugs
Inkle Loom Weaving
Needlepoint Simplified
Patchwork and Other Quilting
Practical Encyclopedia of Crafts
Sewing Without a Pattern
Very Basic Book of Sewing, Altering and
Mending

Photographs by André Bouillaud, Michel Holsnyder,
Claude Jozefson, Philippe Leroy, Georges Rucki,
Pierre-Gilles Solvit, and Edi Vogt.

Drawings by the author.

Translated by Walter A. Simson.

Adapted by Louisa B. Hellegers.

Originally published in France under the title
"Le patchwork" © 1976 by Dessain et Tolra, Paris.

Photographs © 1975, 1974, 1973, 1972 by *Elle*.

Contents

Introduction

Opposite page:
Illus. 1. This charming country landscape in bloom measures about 3 feet by 3 feet (.87 metres by .80 metres). It was made by Béatrice Robelot.

Illus. 2 (right). Made with softly colored cotton prints and solids, this simple design is the work of Jeanne Wallard.

Patchwork, one of the simplest uses of cloth ever conceived, consists of many pieces of fabric sewn together side by side to form a multi-colored whole. It can be composed of complex geometric patterns, or a scattering of abstract and irregular forms. Patchwork allows you to use uneven scraps of cloth that are too small to be used otherwise. The type of cloth you use really doesn't matter: the miracle of creation comes from the many shapes, colors and patterns that are possible. Each finished patchwork is a unique piece which conveys the thought, creativity and patience that you put into it.

As the dazzling and colorful photos* throughout this book show, patchwork is a craft that can take many forms. You, too, can make beautiful works like these with certain basic skills.

* Works made by the candidates of the "Golden Needles" exhibition of the French magazine *Elle* from 1972–1975.

Illus. 3. This classic pattern is entitled "Tulip Lady Fingers." It is from the collection of Mrs. Diane Armand-Delille.

Illus. 4. This pattern is called "Eight-Pointed Star." It is from the collection of Mrs. Diane Armand-Delille.

History

Illus. 5. This is another antique patchwork from the collection of Mrs. Diane Armand-Delille. The oak-leaf like pattern has no name.

Patchwork is an ancient art form. There is evidence of animal-skin patchwork in ancient Egypt, and of more sophisticated patchwork costumes in Japan. As a matter of fact, patchwork art was practiced in every part of the world. But, patchwork as we know it is basically an American craft. Around 1800, immigrants coming to North America from England and Holland had no way to get cloth or clothing. They had to save and use

*Illus. 6. This Canadian patch-
work, owned by Mrs. Ollivary,
is a classic "Log Cabin" pattern. It is composed of half
squares which form, because
of the alternating light and dark
patches, an attractive and regular geometric design.*

every scrap they had. The women organized work sessions to use all the scraps on hand, no matter how small. And they found that they could socialize while they hand-worked their quilts. Finally, a tradition of quilting bees—quilting parties—was started.

The patchwork tradition was indeed a demanding one: a girl's dowry had to include 12 quilts. A 13th was started during the engagement party itself and had to be finished in time for the wedding. The whole family participated in this undertaking. The girls learned to sew fine and regular stitches at an early age, so they could make more complicated quilts later.

Even the quilt names show the influence

of tradition. The names of certain patterns were changed according to current events: for example, "Job's Tears" became "Slave Chain"; then, at the time of the annexation of Texas, "Texas Tears." Finally it was called "Kansas Rocky Road," or, more simply, "Kansas Troubles." Others were called "The Defeat of the Whigs" and "Yankee Pride."

Illus. 7. This classic "Log Cabin" patchwork is presented by Jonathan Holstein.

Illus. 8.

Illus. 9.

Some Traditional Quilt Motifs

Some of the patchwork motifs shown in this chapter are related to well known, traditional quilt designs, each often having its own name or names. Traditional quilt patterns can be known by several different names, depending on their region of origin. So, as you read this chapter, keep in mind that the motif name here is not the only one possible for any design. Of course, the designs drawn or pictured here will appear slightly different from your final results; this is because of the different-patterned fabrics you will use.

You can copy any of the various patterns as they appear here, or you can use them as starting points for creating your own designs. You can use various pattern shapes in different geometric layouts—all side by side, or differently spaced; you can change their order to create a new symmetry; or you can alter the size and scale of a design—enlarge it for a single, giant motif, or divide the surface to construct a pattern of large and small motifs.

Opposite page:
Illus. 8 (top), entitled "Royal Star," and Illus. 9 (bottom), entitled "Rocky Mountain Road," are both from the collection of Mrs. Diane Armand-Delille.

Illus. 11. Solids, prints, laces and ribbons animate this colorful landscape created by Isabelle Durif. It measures about 54 inches by 38 inches (1.45 metres by .95 metres).

Opposite page :
Illus. 10. This charming treehouse, perched and hidden in the woods, is a wonderful reminder of childhood dreams. Measuring about 32 inches by 43 inches (.80 metres by 1.11 metres), this appliquéd patchwork was made by Jocelyne d'Hervez.

Illus. 12. "Star of Bethlehem."

"Star of Bethlehem"

This geometric motif has a subtle optical effect similar to a paper cutout that you first fold in two, then in four, then in a triangle into which you make a few scissor snips to create a magnificent rosette.

You can put the "Star of Bethlehem" on a square background (as shown here) or you can use it as the central design on a bedspread. You can choose a color scheme for your quilt to harmonize with the colors of a certain room, or you can cheer up a room with a multi-colored creation.

The "Star of Bethlehem" is an appliquéd quilt made up of eight diamond-shaped blocks (a block is a repeated motif), each formed of 49 small diamonds and a central motif, with eight arrows (each composed of three dark and three light arrows) connecting the diamond blocks.

The different shades of black, white and grey you see in the drawing emphasize the symmetry of the motif. In your quilt, you should use the same fabrics at the same levels of the diamonds, and make the colors of adjoining levels contrast to make the arrows between the eight blocks stand out. You should try not to let the background fabric show at the middle of the design, because this could disturb the symmetry of the star.

If you're making this patchwork for a bedspread, the star motif should be as wide as or a little less wide than the bed so that the drape of the bedspread does not disturb the position of the star.

The border shown in the drawing straddles the edges of the bedspread, away from the points of the star. This helps you to add the backing when you have finished the rest of the work. If you want to quilt the work, you can follow the outline of the star, or choose different points of the design to stuff. (See the chapter *Quilting and Knotting* on page 79.)

If you don't want to make a bedspread, you can sew the "Star of Bethlehem" onto a simple square background (as in the drawing) for a fascinating wall hanging.

Illus. 13. The ripening fruits on this creative appliquéd tree are really houses. The work, by Bernard Donay, measures about 40 inches by 50 inches (1.15 metres by 1.45 metres).

Illus. 14. This glance out the window combines some touches of embroidery with fabric appliqué. Created by Sylvie Lehman, the hanging measures about 28 inches by 40 inches (.71 metres by 1.05 metres).

Illus. 15. This appliquéd work is embroidered onto a woollen background which adds a special rhythm to the creation. It was made in Holland by Silla Vonkletzing and is about 35 inches by 45 inches (.87 metres by 1.17 metres).

Illus. 16. "Crazy Quilt" worked in strips.

"Crazy Quilt" Worked in Strips

Working in strips allows you to make an unusual surface with uniform sections, each consisting of many differently shaped, colorfully patterned fabric scraps randomly sewn together. This "Crazy Quilt" technique could certainly be the forerunner of some types of modern abstract painting.

This pattern is not appropriate if you want a central background design, but it is suitable for an exciting bedspread. If you do want to make a bedspread, you can stuff each vertical strip individually to give it some body. The amount of body that results depends on the thickness of stuffing you use between the quilted part of the crazy quilt and its backing. (See the chapter *Quilting and Knotting* on page 79.)

To make a "Crazy Quilt," you first make the vertical sections. Choose your fabric scraps and then sew them together using a sewing machine. Stitch each patch to the adjoining ones, leaving about $\frac{1}{2}$ inch (1 cm.) seam allowance on each piece.

When you have made as many strips as you need, carefully baste them together in line with each other. Then sew them together on the underside.

Here, too, you should attach a border that straddles the entire perimeter of the bedspread. This helps hold the patchwork to the backing, holds the stuffing in place if you decide to add it, and gives the colored disorder a uniform finish. (See the chapter *Borders* on page 84.)

You can use this "Crazy Quilt" method to make decorative cushions, too. Since the surface of a cushion is not as big as a bedspread, you don't need to add the single border piece to tie it together. But, you can add a beautiful finishing touch by accenting each edge of the sewn patches with embroidery stitches (chain stitches, buttonhole stitches, herringbone stitches or cross stitches, for instance) done with embroidery thread that is visible against the patchwork. This outline adds delicacy to the cushion, and transforms a simple arrangement of colors into an exceptional work.

Illus. 18. If only the real skyscrapers in our cities could have the charm and balance of the ones in this composition! Created by Jacqueline Martin, this hanging measures about 32 inches by 22 inches (.82 metres by .58 metres).

Opposite page:
Illus. 17. This spectacular square is a close-up of only one of the nine masterpieces which make up the patch-work quilt shown on page 77.

Illus. 19. "North Carolina Lily."

"North Carolina Lily"

This old-fashioned motif, which dates from the time of the American plantation period, is reminiscent of the tranquillity that inspired the pattern. But, the simple and peaceful design demands a lot of work and patience if you want to make it to cover an entire bedspread. You would have to make about 20 similar blocks to appliqué onto a foundation cloth, which could be a simple piece of white cotton. The quilting itself—sketched lightly in the drawing—is similar to the extraordinarily fine and complicated quilt patterns that decorated old quilts made in the "great age of patchwork."

If you have the time and the patience to do these two complementary processes (appliquéing and quilting) at the same time, you can make an incomparable patchwork quilt.

You need four pieces to make each flower. The fabric can be either the same shade or different shades, but to follow the classic motif, you should make the leaves and stems green. The geometric, floral part of the design can be any color or combination of colors you choose. Even outlandish, modern color combinations won't take away from the overall impression of quiet that the bedspread creates.

Traditionally, this quilt is framed with a border of single triangles, whose points face the middle of the quilt and whose colors repeat those of the floral motifs.

You can also arrange the "North Carolina Lily" floral designs in a quilted gridwork you make in a color that contrasts the foundation, or in a ribbon gridwork similar to the one in the "Caesar's Crowns" design shown on page 107. If you do this, you will not need to use triangles for a border, because you can use alternating strips of the same material all around to create the gridwork, letting the foundation material show through them.

Illus. 20. This sunny valley was appliquéd by Françoise Bonvalet. It measures about 24 inches by 20 inches (.61 metres by .51 metres).

Illus. 21. This colorfully blazing appliquéd and embroidered forest fire is the work of Juliette Charrol. It measures about 24 inches by 18 inches (.60 metres by .48 metres).

Illus. 22. Entitled "My House," this lovely patchwork consists of leather and suede appliquéd onto chiné. Created by Anne Scriban, it measures about 30 inches by 23 inches (.76 metres by .58 metres).

Illus. 23. This is a close-up of a Polynesian Tifaifai appliqué.

Illus. 24. This is a close -up of a work en-titled "Double Tifaifai."

Traditional Techniques

As you may have noticed from the quilt descriptions in the preceding chapter, there are basically three different traditional patchwork techniques: mosaic, appliqué and crazy patch.

Mosaic Quilts

In mosaic quilts, many fabric scraps make up the background. To make a mosaic quilt, you must choose fabrics of the same thickness. Then, you must cut and assemble all the odd-shaped pieces very precisely.

If you choose very simple shapes (squares or rectangles, for instance), you can sew them together using your sewing machine. (Assembly details are given in later chapters.)

Appliquéd Quilts

To make an appliquéd quilt, cut different pieces of fabric into certain shapes and hem them so that they have a clean outline. You then sew these pieces, with small, close stitches, onto a visible background cloth whose shape and size determine what the finished project will be.

The Polynesians use the appliqué technique to make *Tifaifai*, charming, native bedspreads whose designs are placed on a single foundation cloth. Usually, the designs are inspired by Polynesian plant life—breadfruit trees, in particular—and consist of bright dashes of color that are characteristic of contemporary abstracts. Illus. 25 shows an example of a *Tifaifai*.

Illus. 25. Here, some Polynesian women are working on Tifaifai—*colorful appliquéd bedspreads with typically native designs.*

The appliqué technique allows you to create decorative, abstract tapestries—real cloth paintings—as well as representational pictures. Illus. 26 and 109 show some examples of appliqué designs. Illus. 26 shows a traditional American design, called "Scrap Basket," with a stylized floral effect. If this idea inspires you, you can make a similar patchwork on a foundation of quilted cotton. The diamonds you choose for the pattern can be of any material, as long as you use the same kind throughout. You can add to the richness of the whole quilt by choosing different prints or calicos for the pattern. Remember that even though this pattern is a classic, it's your choice of fabrics that makes your patchwork unique and personal.

Now, let's look at another pattern. It's the one on page 107 called "Caesar's Crowns." The background consists of a ribbon-like gridwork in between which you sew (by hand or machine) the decorative design. You can work this quilt in one of two ways:

● By appliquéing fine fabric onto an equally fine foundation, and then by attaching this to a thickness of padding or quilt filling (called cotton batting) and to a backing. You join the three layers by quilting tiny stitches that cross the whole piece to form their own design as well as enrich the appliqué design. This traditional quilting method takes a long time to do, but the results are incomparable (see page 79).

● By appliquéing cotton, such as printed calico or gingham, to a quilted foundation. You can make the squares by quilting with thread whose color contrasts with the background. For example, you can do the background in white quilting, the gridwork in sky-blue quilting and the middle designs multi-colored. You can hold all three layers (the foundation, cotton batting and backing) together by making some quilting stitches at strategic places throughout the design.

Illus. 26. This is a drawing of a traditional design,"Scrap Basket."

Crazy-Patch Quilts

Crazy-patch quilts are a combination of irregular pieces. The patches are always different sizes, shapes and colors, and make a dazzling pattern when sewn together. In the old-fashioned quilts, intricate embroidery work often hid the ordinary seam stitches.

Crazy patch was sometimes done by sewing bands of fabric scraps and then by attaching the bands parallel to each other to give a bit of rhythm to the apparent disorder (see Illus. 16).

You could compare crazy-patch quilts to ancient Roman terraces that were tiled with oddly shaped stones. There, grass linked the stones of the terrace much like embroidery links the material of a quilt.

Now that you have some idea of the types of quilts you can make, it's time to learn *how* to make them.

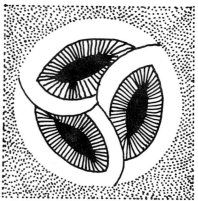

Materials

Whether you choose to create traditional patchwork quilts, or to use the patchwork techniques in unconventional or original ways, the most important ingredient besides your imagination is the "bag of treasures" from which you choose your materials. The charm of patchwork is like a kaleidoscope—the possibilities are infinite. And the more varied your treasure bag of scraps, the more striking and unique will be your creations.

Illus. 27. Collecting a "bag of treasures"—an assortment of different fabrics—is a fun as well as important aspect of creating patchworks. The more varied and unique your choice of fabrics, the more unusual and striking will be your creations.

Illus. 28. This humorous bird, a unique creation made of old neckties, was hatched from the imagina-tion of Simone Hervier. It measures about 47 inches by 32 inches (1.20 metres by .80 metres).

Illus. 29. Here's another amusing bird. Notice that clothing labels make up its feathery tail! Véronique Cossic created this colorful masterpiece.

Opposite page:
Illus. 30. This marvelous farm is teeming with people, animals, trees and flowers. Masterfully created by Anne Trotereau, it measures about 39 inches by 40 inches (1.01 metres by 1.04 metres).

Illus. 31. What city does this delicate picture bring to your mind? By Mireille Hornival.

Do you already have a "bag of treasures" full of different scraps? If you never throw anything out and keep everything in the crazy hope of someday using it, and especially if you sew often, you probably already have a diversity of materials at your disposal. Should you complete your assortment by adding some basic materials, or should you make your patchworks from bits and pieces of everything? Both! Just remember that the success of any work depends on the proper selection of the patch materials.

A good place to start searching for exciting scraps is in your family attic or storage room where you can find some amazing surprises to use as starting points

for a patchwork. For instance, you can use old neckties to create fine results. Look at the patchwork in Illus. 28 that incorporated a great variety of old ties to make a marvelous decorative mural! Patchwork can stimulate your imagination into thinking of using such things as a bow tie on the bird, and other bow ties as butterflies in the background.

Consider the outlines of a fabric floral motif, the circle of an old sleeve, the edges of a small hat that has seen better days—all materials for a large imaginary flower opening its petals after you make just a few quick scissor snips. And why not use an old, outmoded dress that has become too short or too tight, or the body of a man's shirt whose collar is frayed beyond repair, or what's left of a child's overalls whose knees are worn out from rough play, or the pants legs that allowed an out-dated pair of trousers

Illus. 32. What a striking contrast between the black cat and the white lace background behind it! Isabelle Durif originated this squinting-cat portrait, which measures about 35 inches by 27 inches (.78 metres by .68 metres).

Illus. 33. This fish-flower pillow, made of delicately embroidered felt appliqués, is the work of Marie-Madeleine Olive-Diguimont. It measures about 24 inches by 24 inches (.63 metres by .63 metres).

to become a brand-new pair of shorts? Look in the linen closet, too, for holey sheets and pillowcases you can adapt. Put anything you find that might be useful into your bag of treasures.

If you're determined to try your hand at a picture patchwork, but your bag of treasures is still a bit skimpy, don't forget to look for attractive old fabrics at thrift shops, flea markets, garage sales, the Salvation Army or other charitable organizations, or at clothing stores that have "irregulars" or "seconds" on sale.

You can also beg for scraps at your friends' houses. When a friend recognizes her dress that's become a bird of paradise, or his shirt transformed into an attractive many-sided star, you'll feel an even greater sense of accomplishment.

One thing to keep in mind in your search

for scraps is that the fabric must meet certain basic standards, depending on what you decide to make. Will your patchwork be used every day? If so, it should be washable. Will it be a decorative wall hanging? Then dry-cleaning will be necessary to clean it without tearing or otherwise disturbing the patterns.

If you choose washable fabrics, you must wash and iron the pieces before incorporating them into your patchwork. Certain so-called "washable" fabrics shrink upon their first washing, and it's important to be sure that they'll keep their exact dimensions. Woollens must be damp-ironed—that is, ironed with a hot iron and a very damp cloth—before starting.

For a uniform composition, it's best to use the same kind of material throughout, that is, all cotton, all wool, and so on.

Illus. 34. Striking colors and patterned fabrics comprise this surreal landscape by Lorraine Borgeaud. It measures about 50 inches by 28 inches (1.37 metres by .69 metres).

Following is a description of some recommended fabrics for patchwork.

Cotton is ideal to use for patchwork. There are many types of cotton you can choose, such as madras, gingham, chintz, poplin, calico and even cotton blends. All have a fine, closely woven texture that makes them easy to cut and fold, all keep their shape, don't slide, and hardly unravel, if at all.

Quilted cotton, which is thicker, is slightly more difficult to work with, but it lets you maintain the uniform firmness of a quilt

Illus. 35. Here, a tiger-striped cat sleeps peacefully in a spot overlooking his cheerfully colorful home village. This scene was made by Marthe Caillaud.

Illus. 36. Jute canvas provides an excellent rustic-type background for this grouping of exotic wild birds. This appliquéd and embroidered work was created by Vallantin Dulac. It measures about 38 inches by 53 inches (.95 metres by 1.13 metres).

without having to stuff all of the sections yourself.

Burlap and *canvas* come in different degrees of coarseness. Try to avoid using wide weaves (very coarse types) for small pieces, because they unravel very easily, and form uneven edges that are unsightly and difficult to work with.

Jute canvas, for example, is more appropriate for the background of a patchwork project, even though some people like to use it for appliqués in more contemporary works. Note that jute canvas can shrink, and you should, therefore, use it only as the foundation of a wall hanging or other project that won't need to be washed.

Illus. 37. The three-dimensional effect of a tree extending beyond the edges of the background adds special charm to this burlap creation by Claude Joly. The village landscape measures about 28 inches by 15 inches (.72 metres by .35 metres).

Woollens are rich fabrics, infinitely varied in their weaves, their textures and their thicknesses. You can use woollens to achieve particularly warm results.

Some woollens unravel easily and are, therefore, difficult to work with. Thus, try to use finer woollens or tweeds with fine or medium weaves.

You can really appreciate the type of texture you can create with wools if you look at the cat in Illus. 38. Its color and texture contrast especially well with the décor of the background.

Felt is readily available in a wide spectrum of colors in department stores and specialty crafts and fabric shops. Because it is easy to cut into any shape and doesn't need to be hemmed (the edges don't ravel), felt is an especially good fabric to use for patchwork.

Velvet, velour and *corduroy* are good to use for patchwork. You can use their different and contrasting textures to create unique decorative patches with surprising optical effects.

Corduroy comes in a wide variety of

Illus. 38. The distinctive stripes on this primitive cat are simply part of the pattern of the wool chosen by the artist, Michèle Loiselet. The multi-patterned creation measures about 18 inches by 24 inches (.49 metres by .63 metres).

Illus. 39. Wafting smoke from the chimney blends subtly into a fantasy-like forest of free-flowing wools. This dream-like composition was created by Marcel Chikhanovitch and measures about 43 inches by 47 inches (1.16 metres by 1.26 metres).

"wales," from no-wale, which is practically smooth, to very wide-wale, which has widely spaced ribs throughout.

The direction you place a piece of velvet or velour also affects its overall textured appearance. When you use velvet, velour or corduroy, if you change the direction of the grain of two adjacent pieces, you create the impression of varying color intensities. The result is a subtle and attractive rhythm.

It's surely easier to place all the pieces of the same color in the same surface direction, but you can create some outstanding and exciting patches if you experiment. For example, imagine a group of concentric squares, each placed inside the next, and each having finer and finer wales or having alternating directions as they approach the middle. Depending on the colors you choose, you can create a truly extraordinary perspective effect.

You can use this kind of pattern especially well on pillows and cushions, because you can put one pattern on each pillow. If you repeat the patterns on a large surface, you could create a large wall hanging. Imagine, for example, the drawing in Illus. 110 done with different textures of corduroy, velvet or velour rather than with different printed fabrics.

The imaginative creation in Illus. 40 uses the wales of the corduroy in distinct and different directions to suggest the furrows of plowed earth.

Silk allows you to make very delicate and refined patchworks. Because of its light weight, you sometimes have to pad silk or add a backing before sewing pieces of it

Illus. 41. Soft and delicate colors and patterns of silk resulted in this lovely sunset by Martine Hubert. The masterpiece measures about 45 inches by 35 inches (1.21 metres by .89 metres).

Illus. 42. Flamboyant satins and other shiny fabrics evoke the era of the Roaring Twenties in this marvelous work by Mireille Mornival. The embroidered appliquéd patchwork measures about 30 inches by 36 inches (.76 metres by .88 metres).

together. You can use colorful Indian silk scarves, which are widely available today, to complete an arrangement of silks in an exquisite cushion, or a scene composed of delicate prints (see Illus. 41).

Satin and other shiny fabrics are rarely used in patchwork, but they do look remarkably well in shimmering scenes, like the one of the Roaring Twenties shown in Illus. 42.

Lace, because of its patterns, openness and daintiness, lends itself well to perfectly charming effects in patchwork creations. You can use pieces of lace alone or together with other more opaque materials to form either the base of a work, or to lighten a project with a few well placed pieces.

Illus. 43 shows a lovely project, made by a man, Gérard Capuano, that really proves that delicate lacework can be used to create a striking effect.

Illus. 43. Beautiful scraps of various laces were artistically arranged by Gérard Capuano to create this superb and delicate patchwork.

Lamé and sequinned fabrics were chosen by the makers of the patchworks in Illus. 46 and 47 to highlight their work by drawing attention to certain points of composition. Illus. 47 shows that even young children can create charming patchworks. (Rainy days or holidays can become fascinating for those who know patchwork!)

Buttons and other fasteners were not used by the early traditional quilters, but they have every right to be considered for creative purposes—their raised, colored effects can add much to contemporary patchwork.

The forms and colors of simple buttons can easily spark your imagination. They can be fruit hanging from a tree, borders of your character's clothes, scales of a fish, hearts of flowers and much more. In Illus. 45, for

Illus. 46. Lamé and other scintillating fabrics comprise this striking masterpiece by Béatrice Robelot.

example, the buttons define and enliven this very beautiful piece where fantasy is combined with a well ordered design.

If you decide to use buttons for a quilt or a bedspread, make sure they are firmly attached to a thick stuffing in which they'll lie; otherwise, they might be pulled off if someone sits on the bed.

Illus. 47. Lamé and other cheerfully colored fabrics were imaginatively used by Stephan Testanière to produce this enchanting appliquéd patchwork. Even children can attain marvelous results using the techniques and ideas described in this book.

Buckles, snap fasteners, rings and other metal bric-a-brac can also suggest imaginary objects (a knight's spurs, a fence in the countryside, the details of a suit of armor, and so on). You can create fanciful contrasts if you make part of a wall hanging in the more traditional way, and part using such interesting additions.

Ribbon, braid and trim can enhance your creativity enormously. Ribbon allows you to make attractive geometric compositions with parallel bands. The interplay of the different widths, numerous patterns and varying textures available offers you endless possibilities. Because ribbons have bound edges, you can experiment with them without having to hem them. Also, if a particular piece of ribbon is a bit wide, you can cut it

Illus. 48. This marvelous, stylized nature scene was created with spectacular ribbons, felt and other bright fabrics by Madeleine Ducou. It measures about 32 inches by 43 inches (.79 metres by 1.11 metres).

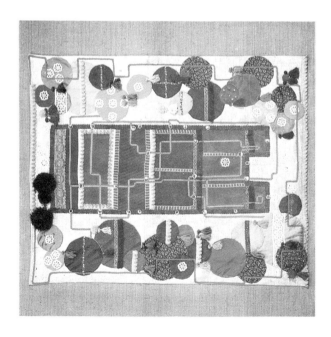

Illus. 49. Do you see an aerial view of a house surrounded by the trees of its garden in this creation? Various trims and fabric scraps were imaginatively utilized by M. E. Chaix to construct this unique floor plan.

into squares, rectangles, diamonds or any other geometric shape you want.

There are many different kinds of trim you can use to add a three-dimensional quality to your patchwork. They can bring life and charm to your decorative pictures, but you have to remember that they're a bit fragile, especially in the wash. Just be sure they are firmly attached to your project and they will stay intact.

Illus. 50. An assortment of trims, ribbons and pompons make this patchwork appliqué come alive. Created by Joëlle Tardieu, it measures about 28 inches by 28 inches (.70 metres by .72 metres).

Tools

Before you begin to work on a project, you should gather all the tools you'll be using. You can find most of the necessary tools listed below in your regular sewing basket:

- A pair of very sharp scissors, so there's no risk of ruining a delicate piece of fabric when you cut it.
- A pair of heavy-duty scissors for cutting templates out of cardboard.
- A single-edge razor blade or X-acto knife or some such tool.
- A thimble.
- A set of sewing needles.
- Pins (preferably metal ones, because their fineness minimizes holes in the fabric).

- Basting thread.
- Sewing thread to sew the patches together. You should have at least some black and some white thread; use the black thread for sewing dark fabrics, and the white for light ones. Remember that when you sew a light fabric to a dark fabric, your fine stitches will be less visible if you sew them with black thread. Actually, it's best if you try to match the color of the thread to the color of the patch. If you sew often, you've probably already accumulated many colors in your sewing basket. Stitch silk patchworks with silk thread.
- Some embroidery thread if you decide

Illus. 52. This tranquil scene was created in Quebec by Geneviève Deronzière. The appliquéd elements are outlined with embroidery in this lovely hanging which measures about 30 inches by 40 inches (.77 metres by 1.04 metres).

Opposite page:
Illus. 51. Contrasting black embroidery around each patch highlights the bold areas of color in this fabulous fabric painting by Françoise Schneider.

Illus. 53. The simple tools pictured here, plus some cardboard and paper, are all you need to begin working on your creative patchworks.

to outline the patches of your patchwork by embroidering a visible border, as was done in Illus. 51 and 52. "Crazy quilts" were often made like this, out of bits of scrap, each one outlined in different embroidery stitches.

● An iron and a damp cloth for damp-ironing.

● Cardboard, transparent tape and tracing paper.

● A ruler, a pencil and tailor's chalk for marking dark fabrics.

● Oaktag or Bristol board or shoe-box cardboard, old notebook covers, or some other similar-weight cardboard.

● For smaller designs, you need some graph paper, which makes tracing simple geometric figures much easier. These figures form the basis of traditional patchwork designs: squares, rectangles, diamonds, pentagons, octagons, triangles, hexagons, and circles.

With all these materials now at hand, you can begin your patchwork.

Planning a Patchwork

Laying Out a Design

Your first task is to choose a design. The designs scattered throughout this book, and especially those in the chapter beginning on page 102, are simply sketches that you can easily adapt in any way you want. When shown alone, some designs don't al-ways give you a good idea of what they could look like when placed either in rows or in groups of four concentric squares. Illus. 54 and 55 give you an idea of how this repetition works.

Try your own hand at drawing some geo-

Illus. 54 (below) and Illus. 55 (right). By repeating a simple design as a larger design composed of four concentric squares, as is shown here, you can create many interesting and suitable motifs for patchworks.

Illus. 56. If you choose a simple geometric shape, and cut several samples of it from colored paper, you can easily experiment and discover an endless variety of pleasing designs.

metric designs—the possibilities are endless. Use pieces of colored paper to test out pleasing patterns. As you create various motifs and combine them in different ways, you will surely discover some very exciting patterns. After experimenting a bit, choose a motif or design you like enough to enlarge or repeat for an entire quilt.

Illus. 57. Re-arrange your sample shapes as many times as you want—until you create the arrangement that you like the best.

Illus. 58 (above left), Illus. 59 (below left), Illus. 60 (above right) and Illus. 61 (below right). Notice the great diversity of patterns you can create using just one simple geometric design.

Illus. 62. The alternating directions and contrasting patterns of the diagonal strips which make up each square of this patchwork add to its overall balance. The decorative border unifies the entire piece, created by Eliane Métral.

Deciding Basic Proportions

Theoretically, the size of each patch should somehow correspond to the larger dimensions of the project. It's simple: a smaller project should be made up of small pieces, and a larger one of large pieces.

For example, use patches which are less than 4 inches (10 cm.) on a side to make a bag, a cushion, a vest or a toy; use patches between 4 and 6 inches (10–15 cm.) or more for a large surface, such as a bedspread or a large wall hanging.

Illus. 62 is a beautiful example of a geometric quilt in which the different blocks are in classic proportion to the whole. Each square consists of diagonal strips. The whole design is co-ordinated by an important

decorative border which contrasts the center colors.

But, you don't have to follow any absolute rules of proportion in your patchworks. A handbag made of four large squares would be fun to make and a long skirt livened up with a few large diamonds or rectangles would be really stylish. And, you certainly wouldn't worry about proportion if you created a bedspread from a mosaic of many tiny pieces. In fact, many older quilts were made from many mosaic pieces, and the effect of these quilts is highly decorative.

There is, then, really no hard and fast rule concerning proportion. You should just remember that a surface appears larger when divided into smaller sections. For example, if you'd like to make a skirt, you should know that the smaller you make the patches, the larger the wearer's figure will appear. Larger designs, on the other hand, seem to reduce the figure.

Also remember that you can slim a figure by framing a central patchwork panel with two sides of a dark material.

Illus. 63. Despite the abundance of grey in this appliquéd picture, these chickens still come to life as they peck at their food. Brigitte Grandry created this basically monochromatic farm scene which measures about 45 inches by 37 inches (1.15 metres by .92 metres).

Illus. 64. A reminder of a vacation setting— whether real or imaginary—can add spark to a city home all year round. This vacation home was made by Anne Cantenot and measures about 28 inches by 19 inches (.73 metres by .51 metres).

Choosing a Color Scheme

Your next task is to choose a color scheme. This depends, in part, on what you've got in your bag of treasures. Your choice of colors, of course, should harmonize with or complement the colors of the room the quilt is intended for (unless you're treating the project as a painting with a specific spot in mind). Basically monochromatic or single-color compositions can also be beautiful, as Illus. 63 and Illus. 65 show. But don't hesitate to experiment with bright and unusual color and pattern combinations either. Sometimes, colors or patterns you would never consider compatible look superb when combined in a patchwork. You can create exotic results if you choose imaginative mixes of colorfully patterned fabrics.

Illus. 65. This gorgeous abstract was created by Monique Graf of Switzerland. It measures about 32 inches by 47 inches (.80 metres by 1.20 metres).

Illus. 66. This immense floral motif ornaments a bedspread which is about 47 inches by 90 inches (1.20 metres by 2.26 metres). The magnificent flower stands out against the sunburst background of printed cottons. Josette Roubin is the artist.

57

Preparing the Patches

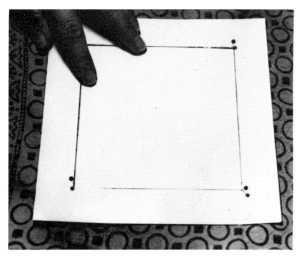

Illus. 67. To center a patterned design, first make a template about ½ inch (1 cm.) larger than the true size you need. Then score the true outline as shown.

Once you have chosen a particular shape or shapes for your patches, and a general color scheme, you should make sure you have enough fabric to cut the right number of patches to cover the planned surface.

Now, you have to cut out templates (patterns) from cardboard. (The example used here to illustrate the patchwork techniques is a simple figure—the square.) Cut out a cardboard square to the exact dimensions of the patch you decided upon. Then, leaving about ½ inch (1 cm.) extra around the edges of the template (for a seam allowance), cut out a square from the fabric.

If you want to center your design to correspond with the print of your fabric, here is how to do it using the template: trace around the template exactly onto some cardboard. Now, re-draw the shape around your tracing leaving an extra ½ inch (1 cm.). Cut

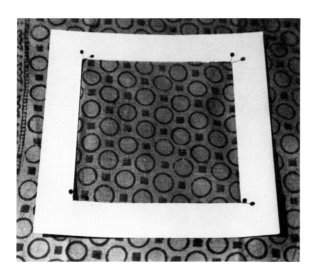

Illus. 68 (left) and Illus. 69 (right). You end up with a cardboard frame that lets you center any motif.

Illus. 70. This shows the reverse side of a patch. Basting criss-crossed stitches from one edge to the one opposite helps hold the fabric in place around the template.

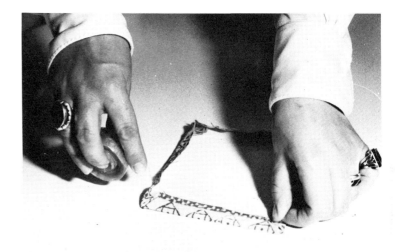

Illus. 71. You can use transparent tape instead of basting stitches to hold the fabric in place around the template.

out the cardboard following the outline of the larger drawing. Then cut out the true template shape by scoring and cutting the inner tracing with a single-edge razor blade or similar tool.

You now have a cardboard frame that lets you center your design on the fabric as you look through this "open window." When you cut out the fabric, follow the larger outline.

After you have cut out the patches, you must hem each one all the way around by tucking the top under to follow the true outline of the template. If you place the frame on the surface first, you can easily mark the corners of the template by sticking pins into the fabric at the corners. This helps you fold under the fabric. To make sure the folds follow the border of the template, you should flatten the hem by ironing over it with a

Illus. 72. If you have a steady hand, you can simply damp-iron the fabric around the template. Using a little spray starch ensures an even edge.

Illus. 73. This brilliant bedspread, designed and created by Rita Endt, shows a truly unique adaptation of a simple geometric shape—the square. This colorful patchwork measures about 58 inches by 86 inches (1.50 metres by 2.20 metres).

Illus. 74. Tablecloth with appliquéd fabrics by Claire Hartmann. 39 inches by 39 inches (1.20 metres by 1.20 metres).

Opposite page:
Illus. 75. Bright and cheerful cottons and satins comprise this charming and juvenile aquatic design by Jacqueline Duvernoy. The work measures about 37 inches by 26 inches (.95 metres by .64 metres).

damp cloth. This is easier to do if you first baste from one edge of the underside to the other to hold the form well in place (see Illus. 70). You can use some transparent tape instead of the basting thread to attach the hem to the cardboard (see Illus. 71).

If you have a steady hand, you can damp-iron the fold without this kind of preparation. If you do, you can ensure an even edge if you use some spray starch.

Keep in mind as you work that the hemmed border must correspond exactly with the hem of the adjacent patch, especially for a mosaic quilt. Be sure to avoid any extra overlap—even a fraction of an inch (a few extra millimeters) can easily sneak in one way or another. If this happens on several patches, you can ruin the rhythm and symmetry of the patchwork.

You are now ready to create your patchwork. There are two ways of approaching this task—the simplified technique and the traditional technique. Both methods are discussed in the following chapters.

Making a Patchwork—
the Simplified Technique

A simple way to make a patchwork is to sew the patches together with a sewing machine. This is especially quick if your patches are squares or rectangles, such as for a mosaic patchwork. When you cut out the patches for this method, simply cut each piece along the template by tracing the outline on the back of the fabric (use light-colored chalk on dark fabric or a dark pencil on light fabric). Cut the fabric *with* the grain so that the patches don't pucker when you sew them together, or when you eventually wash the final product.

You don't have to worry so much about the hem when you cut the fabric pieces for machine sewing. After you have experimented, and have decided where you want to place each patch, lay them out in your planned pattern. Then, begin at either the left or the right of your design and stitch along the tracing lines (right sides together). Prepare all the vertical columns in this way.

When you have made as many long strips as you need for your patchwork, carefully loosen the stitches a little on the right side of the fabric, either with an iron or by exerting

a little pressure with your fingernail. This adds some fullness and a natural quality. It also allows you to finish the project where it might be difficult to use an iron.

Now, all that's left is to baste the strips of patches together, making sure that the corners are perfectly matched, and also making sure that you stitch from the top to the bottom of each strip with a single thread.

Again, loosen these stitches with the tip of an iron or your fingernail. You should

be pleased with the quick results—the patchwork part of your project is already assembled!

This simplified technique allows you to make original patchwork backgrounds rather quickly and easily. You can back and trim these creations to make bedspreads, but you can also use your patterns for bags, clothes, toys, shades, pajama bags . . . the list is endless. All you have to do is decide how to finish your piece.

Illus. 76. Bold shapes and large areas of color characterize this primitive farm scene by Marie-Paule Legrand. The appliquéd and embroidered scene measures about 55 inches by 47 inches (1.42 metres by 1.20 metres).

Opposite page:
Illus. 77. Lots of time, patience and artistic inspiration went into the creation of this beautiful patchwork. The individually stuffed leaves add an airy feeling to the tree, while the contrasting dark background and subtly textured surrounding landscape add the perfect complementary effects. Michelle Armeni is the proud artist who constructed this 32-inch by 40-inch (.83-metre by 1.03-metre) masterpiece.

64

Finishing

The simplified machine-stitched patch-work technique also allows you to finish your project quickly. The specific finishing touches you add to a machine-sewn patch-work depend on its type. If you plan to follow a pattern, such as for a toy or article of clothing, simply treat your patchwork as you would any other piece of fabric. Following are some additional ideas.

A Bedspread

If you have made a bedspread, you must choose an attractive backing to complement or harmonize with your patchwork. You can sew the backing to the patchwork in one of several ways. You can simply place the right sides together and sew around all four corners and three sides. Turn the bedspread right-side-out and then stitch the opening by hand. Or, you can keep right-sides-out, turn under a hem all around, and then stitch the entire bedspread together by hand. In either case, you can add a ruffle as you construct the bedspread, or attach an appropriate border as you sew up the sides. (See the chapter *Borders* on page 84 for detailed instructions.)

After the sides are sewn, you should make a few hand stitches through both layers at strategic places in the patchwork design (such as at the middle of a motif) to hold the two layers in place.

A Pillow or Cushion

You can make a decorative throw pillow or cushion in exactly the same way as a bedspread. Because of its smaller size, a pillow is a quick and fun patchwork project. Add the pillow stuffing before you sew the fourth side.

A Quilt

If you want to make a simple bedspread into a heavier, more traditional quilt, all you have to do is add an extra layer of quilt filling—called cotton batting—between the two layers before you sew them together. (See the chapter *Quilting and Knotting* on page 79 for complete, traditional quilting instructions.)

Making a quilt from your patchwork is, obviously, a time-consuming matter, but your final product will be one you can be proud of for years to come.

A Picture or Wall Hanging

You can back a patchwork which you plan to hang up the same way you do a bedspread. Or, you can fringe the edges of the background for an unusual effect. You can also take the finished project to a professional to have it framed.

Illus. 78. Fringing the edges of a wall hanging, as was done on this magnificent piece by M. Deheuse, adds special character to the creation.

Glance through the pages of this book for some original ideas on how to finish your hanging patchwork. (See also the chapter *Hanging a Patchwork Picture* on page 91 for further ideas and specific instructions.)

A Rug

If you want to make a patchwork rug (from heavy, strong fabrics), back it with heavy haircloth. You can attach a strip of trim to the haircloth with hem stitches. Stitch the turned-in edge of the hem to the back of the haircloth—this way no stitches will show.

You can also attach a backing to your patchwork rug by trimming it with rug binding. You must attach the rug to the backing in several places, so that the fabric doesn't fold or bend when people walk on it. In any case, be sure to turn the edges of the binding carefully over the entire thickness of the edges of the heavy backing.

Iron-On Backing

If your patchwork is made of light-weight materials, and you are not concerned with maintaining an entirely hand-crafted charm for your patchwork, you can add some body to it by making an iron-on material into a backing.

Cut the iron-on material to the exact outline of your project. Then place your patchwork right-side-down on a perfectly flat surface. Now flatten the iron-on material on top of the patchwork, making sure that none of the edges are folded. Damp- or steam-iron the backing in place. Dry (if necessary) with a warm iron.

After letting the patchwork cool, cut around its edges, leaving about an inch (2.5 cm.) extra all the way around the iron-on. All that is left to do is finish the edges. If you're making something that has many pieces to sew together (for example, a hand-bag, toy, cushion or vest), you can attach the pieces with hand-stitches or quilting stitches around the outline of the iron-on. Or, you can turn under the edges and embroider them with hem stitches or herringbone stitches.

Making a Patchwork— the Traditional Technique

With the faster, machine-stitched technique discussed in the previous chapter, you can avoid putting each fabric patch around a cardboard template. But, the truly traditional (completely hand-crafted) patchwork technique does require you to follow several additional steps. First, you must trace each patch onto the back of the fabric. Then, you must cut out the fabric, leaving about a ½-inch (1-cm.) seam allowance so that you can whip stitch each patch to the adjacent ones.

The first thing you must decide is what you want to make—a bedspread, pillow or wall hanging, for example—and which patchwork technique you plan to use to create that item. Then draw an appropriate design, keeping in mind what you learned in the chapter *Planning a Patchwork* on page 51.

Transferring Your Drawing

To reproduce your drawing as a patchwork, first transfer each separate piece of the entire drawing onto paper. Then cut out each distinct piece of the composition. Then re-transfer each of these pieces onto cardboard, cut them out and cover them with your fabric, as was discussed on pages 58 to 61.

If your original design is a different size from the size you want your patchwork to be, you can enlarge it or reduce it using the "grid technique." Just draw a gridwork of squares over the original drawing. Then transfer the design to another gridwork—graph paper, for example—whose squares are either larger or smaller than your original, depending on the size you want your final design to be. You simply copy freehand a portion of the design from a square of the original to the corresponding square in the new size. See Illus. 79.

After you have prepared your fabric-covered templates, you should plan your final design.

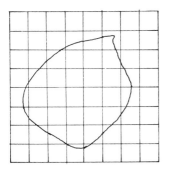

Illus. 79. Use the grid technique, illustrated here, to enlarge or reduce designs for your patchworks.

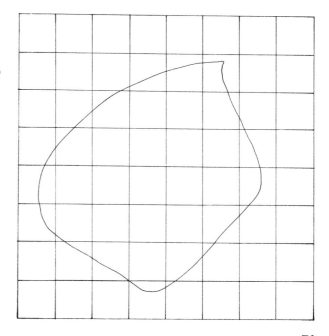

Illus. 80. To lay out your design, leave the cardboard templates attached to the fabric so the various pieces don't lose their shape. You can plan your final design more accurately this way.

Laying Out Your Design

If you are making a mosaic or appliqué patchwork, you really should make templates and damp-iron the hem around them, as described on pages 58 to 61. Leave the cardboard templates attached to the cloth, so that you can experiment with the shapes for the best possible combinations and layout. This way, the pieces won't lose their shape between work sessions, and you can get a clear idea of the shape your finished project will be before you start to cut. You can number the pieces on the back to remind you of their order.

The way you lay out the shapes that will decorate your patchwork is very important. If you are making a bedspread for your own bed, you can spread out the background fabric on the bed and use pins to mark the important areas of your composition. (If you plan to have pillows or bolsters underneath the bedspread, remember to take them into account when you plan the size and pattern.) Later, you can replace the pins with a few basting stitches to make sure the marks stay in place. Depending on the motif you finally choose, you may want to place it in a regular, repeating pattern throughout the whole surface, remembering to leave enough room at the edges for the border. Or, you may want to make a single, central design. If you want to make a particularly modern bedspread, you can put the motifs wherever you want, without worrying about symmetry or a definite pattern.

If you are making a patchwork divided into regular squares or rectangles, divide the surface to be covered so that you have an equal number of shapes in both the height and width. For example, for a bed 56 inches by 76 inches (1.40 by 1.90 metres), you can place five 14-inch (35 cm.) squares along the length, which will leave a 3-inch (7.5 cm.) strip on each end of the bedspread for the border.

If you are planning to include the grid lines in your design, be sure to mark them on the background with large basting stitches, so that you don't forget to account for their width in your final patchwork. Once you have marked the squares on the background, you can determine the ideal position of each of your designs. Just count the number of squares between the design and the edge of the background. For example, to center the design, make sure that there is an equal number of squares on each side of it.

You can use transparent tape to temporarily hold the different parts of your patchwork together. You might especially want to do this if you are making a decorative wall hanging, because it's often hard to judge how you like the placement of the designs unless you see the piece hanging. By using tape, you can change the position of the design elements without having to take the hanging off the wall. This is also a good way to tell if one of the designs isn't exactly fitted to its cardboard template, and you'll save valuable time and avoid frustration if you fix it at this point.

Illus. 81. If you decide to make your templates from paper, be careful not to iron over the pins you use to hold the paper in place. Otherwise, you can leave unsightly, difficult-to-remove impressions in your fabric.

An Alternate Method

There is another possible way of preparing your patches. If you do not want to make the templates from cardboard, you can make them from paper and hold them in place on your chosen fabric with pins or basting stitches before damp-ironing the hem. Make a test on a sample before doing all your pieces this way. Be sure you iron the fold of the fabric at the very edge of the template without flattening the pins or the basting thread, because otherwise you could leave permanent impressions in the fabric.

Assembling the Patchwork

After you have carefully prepared all the pieces in either way you choose, and have decided on their placement, sew them together with fine whip stitches on the underside, or, if you have a little more skill, on the top of the fabric. This hand-stitching is an added charm of the craft. Before you start to sew, make sure that the edges you plan to sew together have the exact same dimensions, and that the corners match precisely. If you made the templates carefully, this should be no problem.

If you are making an appliquéd patchwork and plan to cover the whole foundation surface with appliqués, the pieces should fit together without overlaps or gaps.

In Illus. 82, for example, the outline of the house appliqué contrasts with the background (the sky), even though it is just an

Illus. 82. The elements of a patchwork design need not be fragile or delicate. As you can see in this charming work by Elisabeth Glenconner, big, bold areas of color and pattern can result in a wonderful creation as well.

Illus. 83. Notice how perfectly the edges of each patch in this delicate landscape match those of its adjacent patches. Careful planning while you are making your appliqués adds an expert look to your final creation. This wall hanging is the work of Sylvianne Lude, and measures about 49 inches by 41 inches (1.25 metres by 1.05 metres).

Opposite page:
Illus. 84. Gorgeous colors and magnificently patterned fabrics, as well as patient and intricate work by artist Nellie Louchouarn, resulted in this beautiful patchwork quilt. You can see close-ups of two of the squares on pages 20 and 80.

added layer of cloth, and it didn't require the same precise cutting-out as it would have if it were an appliqué. (You can see another beautiful example of this type of appliqué in Illus. 83.) As you can see, the outline of a design on a single foundation without stitches doesn't necessarily lessen the effect of the patchwork—it just lessens the work involved.

If you used the mosaic technique for your patchwork, you should leave the cardboard or paper templates in place until you have sewn all the patches together.

Then you can carefully remove the basting stitches. Don't do this too fast, or pull the stitches any old way, because you will risk ruining the project if you are not careful.

If you used the appliqué technique, detach the templates after damp-ironing. Pin each patch to the background before attaching it there with hem stitches. You should try to sew the appliqués with thread that is the dominant color of the appliqué.

Depending on the pattern you have chosen, you should split the work into two procedures. Remember that each main design should form a "block" made of many patches. First, put each block together. Then sew all the blocks onto the background. Illus. 84 shows a project which is made of 12 of these blocks.

Because of the many motifs that are possible in patchwork, and because of the great amount of time that is required of a single

craftsperson to make one, patchwork is the type of work that has naturally lent itself to teamwork. Traditionally, people used to meet socially for quilting parties and quilting bees. The different blocks of a large patchwork can be made by different people—an entire school class, a youth group, residents of an old age or convalescent home, even just a group of friends. Then, all you have to do is sew all the different blocks together for the final patchwork. This takes almost as little time as it takes to make a single block, because everyone who contributed can share this work, too.

Finishing

After you have sewn all the patches together, you should iron the project. Don't iron the patches as you sew them, or you will lose the light, natural fluffiness characteristic of hand-sewn patchwork. Instead, you can simply loosen the stitches with your fingernail to equalize the tension on the fabric.

When you have finished ironing the patchwork, you are ready to construct the final product. (See also the finishing instructions and ideas described on pages 66 to 69, as well as in the chapters *Quilting and Knotting* on page 79, *Borders* on page 84, and *Hanging a Patchwork Picture* on page 91.) Since you have followed the traditional hand-crafted method of making this patchwork, remember that your finished project will look more consistent and attractive if you also complete it by hand, rather than on the sewing machine or by using an iron-on backing.

The most important thing you need to do is to choose an appropriate backing. If you don't add a backing, the edges of the many patches can unravel. A backing—even if it is simply a layer of fabric—will give your patchwork an incomparable finish. It should be tailor-made to the exact size of the work. There are two ways to do this:

1. You can turn under the edge of the backing from its right side to its wrong side, and then turn under the perimeter of the patchwork itself in the same way. Then sew the two together back-to-back (right-sides-out). You can sew the edges either with whip stitches that straddle the edge, or with quilting stitches—small, hand-sewn running stitches—as close as possible to the edge.

Or, you can follow another traditional method and fold the backing about an inch (2.5 cm.) over the top and then stitch in place.

Depending on the style and use of the project, you can hide these stitches with chain stitches, or herringbone or spine stitches, done with embroidery floss or silk thread. You can even change the color of the needlework each time you refill the needle. Use your imagination to do this decorative embroidery: anything goes.

2. You can also hold the patchwork and its backing together by adding on a trim (such as a border or a ruffle) that straddles their common edge.

Once your patchwork is backed, there are several ways in which you can complete your project, depending on its size and purpose. The following chapters describe various methods.

Quilting and Knotting

Quilting your patchwork—thereby finishing it in the old tradition of American quilts —adds practical warmth to its hand-crafted beauty. To quilt, you first place a thickness of quilt stuffing—called cotton batting or simply batting—between the patchwork material itself and the backing. Then you sew this layer in place. There are two ways of doing this:

The first way is by *quilting*, which you do

Illus. 85. This appliquéd patchwork, which incorporated overall quilting as part of the beauty of the piece, is from the collection of Mrs. Diane Armand-Delille.

by simply stitching the three thicknesses together using very small running stitches (quilting stitches). You can either follow the outlines of all the patches from the top side, or criss-cross the whole patchwork with an overall quilting, without bothering to outline the designs at all. Illus. 85 is an example of this kind of quilting.

If you want to sew quilting stitches between the blocks of your patchwork, as in the "North Carolina Lily" (Illus. 19) or "Caesar's Crowns" (Illus. 109), all you have to do is draw or trace the design you want to quilt on a piece of tracing paper. Pin the drawing on the top of the quilt and then sew the fine, even stitches through both the paper and all the thicknesses of your quilt. After you have followed the design on the paper, gently pull off the paper. The quilting motif remains, perfectly reproduced on the quilt.

Of course, the stitches that you use to hold the three thicknesses of a quilt together can also be decorative. Each quilting stitch can be a tiny cross—a visible splash of color—that can serve as the focal point of a design, or as part of the rhythm on an already decorated surface.

The second way is by *knotting*, which you do by tying the three thicknesses together with stitches placed at regular intervals—usually at the corners of different patches.

Opposite page:
Illus. 86. This is a close-up of one of the squares shown in the quilt on page 77. If you look closely at the border, you can see the tiny quilting stitches that add traditional and artistic authenticity to this beautifully made appliqué.

You hold each stitch on the back with a double knot (the mattress-stitching on old fashioned mattresses was done this way to keep the wool from bunching, and to make sure the stuffing was well distributed). If you want, you can place the double knot on the top side of the quilt, where, of course, it will show, but it can also add special charm to your design.

Setting Up

Whether you decide to use quilting or knotting, you first have to spread a backing you chose on any large surface—the floor, for example. Be sure to choose a fine quality fabric for the backing of your quilt. After all, the backing *is* a part of your artwork, and it must last for a long time. Then, carefully place the batting on top of the backing, spreading and smoothing it from the center outwards with the palm of your hand. The batting should be a few inches (about 4 to 5 cm.) smaller all around than the backing. You can make some large basting stitches to hold the batting in place; stitch two perpendicular lines through the middle of the backing to the outside edges, and also two diagonal lines through the middle to the corners.

Once you have basted the batting to the backing, you should place and then baste the patchwork itself on top. Be sure not to let even a tiny fold appear in any of the thicknesses of fabric.

The entire procedure just described is much easier to do if you somehow suspend the quilt under some tension. You can either tack the ends of the quilt onto a special wooden quilting frame, or simply hang it

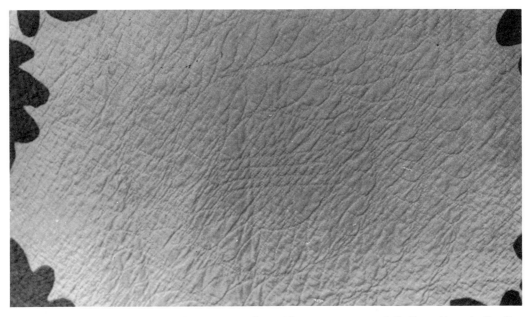

Illus. 87. If you look closely at this portion of a quilt, you can see a definite pattern to the tiny quilting stitches. This is a close-up of a quilt from the collection of Mrs. Diane Armand-Delille.

between two sawhorses, also tacking the edges to secure it.

If you want to use a quilting frame, consult a local crafts shop where you may be able to buy one. Or, you can easily make one using four pieces of 1 × 2 inch (2.5 × 5 cm.) lumber. The easiest way to construct the frame is to use C-clamps to hold the four pieces of wood together at the corners. Then, you simply thumbtack the quilt layers to the frame. Put the backing on first, the batting next, and then your patchwork. If the tension seems too loose, carefully loosen the C-clamps and pull the frame out slightly. You should do this *before* you put the batting on top of the backing.

Then baste the layers in place. When the quilt is on a frame, you really only need to baste the three layers together along all four sides.

Instead of making the special quilting frame to suspend your quilt, you can merely add enough basting stitches to evenly cover and thus hold together the entire surface, and then use a quilting hoop while you quilt.

Quilting and Knotting

Naturally, the thread you use for quilting should be very strong, as you have to pull hard after each stitch. Thread that's either too fine or of inferior quality won't stand up to the job. Never double over ordinary sewing thread for quilting or knotting: it will fray at the eye of the needle and break when you pull the stitch.

Silk thread is just the perfect strength without being too thick. So-called "button thread" is also good. If you want, you can do the quilting with very fine waxed thread. Pearl cotton, which is sold on large spools, is also all right to use.

Make a knot at the end of the thread. To begin, stick the needle through from the back to the front. Gently pull the knot through the backing, so it won't show, and imbed it instead in the batting.

Start to quilt at the middle of the patchwork. Hold the quilt from underneath with your left hand (if you are right-handed). Stitch towards yourself with an under-over, under-over movement, making sure the needle passes perpendicularly through the quilt, and not at an angle. Make the quilting stitches through all three thicknesses, stopping every five or six stitches to pull the thread tight. Add an extra stitch at the end of each piece of thread for extra strength. Then run the end off under the patchwork, into the batting layer.

Go back over your work from time to time, to make sure that the thread is under the right amount of tension. The thread should make a deep indentation in the thickness of the stuffing. The touch of your left hand underneath the quilt indicates whether the needle has gone through all three quilt layers correctly.

Finishing the Edges

After you have completed the quilting, you have to finish off the edges of the backing and patchwork. See page 78 for how to do this. The next chapter, *Borders*, can also give you some ideas.

Borders

American quilts were always trimmed with geometric borders, or with more "romantic" designs repeated all around the edges. Even a very simple border, made from a single piece of fabric, is indispensable to give a patchwork a finished appearance. Illus. 88 shows this well. Illus. 89, on the other hand, shows an example of how a striking geo-

Illus. 88. You can certainly appreciate the importance of a border as a finishing touch in this sprightly patchwork by Andrée Rembry. It measures about 58 inches by 49 inches (1.50 metres by 1.22 metres).

Illus. 89. The geometric motif of the border is only part of the charm of this colorful patchwork. Notice the adorable kitten and baby owl, both stuffed, and both completely independent of the background, so you can actually lift them out. Geneviève Lirda is the imaginative creator of this three-dimensional quilt which measures about 47 inches by 32 inches (1.21 metres by .79 metres).

metric motif can attractively frame the two blocks of the picture.

Like the choice of colors for your patchwork, deciding how to decorate the borders is limited only by your imagination. The sketches of geometric designs in Illus. 90 should give you some ideas. Another good possibility is to repeat one of the shapes from the main design throughout the border.

Regardless of the design or fabric you choose, be sure you cut strips wide enough to fold over the edges of the patchwork top and the backing. Be sure to leave extra for the hem. Also, since the borders must fit

Illus. 90. Here are some geometric designs that you can use in your patchworks or adapt as attractive borders.

exactly at the corners, be sure to cut the border strips carefully and accurately.

Now, calculate the placement of the designs carefully. Sew the designs on, but do not appliqué any motifs onto the four corners until after you have formed the angles by fitting and sewing the borders around the quilt. In this way, you can place the last four designs more exactly in the corners.

Place the border strips around the quilt layers. Turn under a small hem on the top and the backing. Pin or baste the turned-under border in place. When the corners are fitted properly, appliqué the final designs there.

Now, with tiny hem stitches or whip stitches, sew the border to the quilt. You can also use small quilting stitches to do this. Of course, you can sew the border on by machine, but you will certainly lose some of the marvelous, hand-crafted quality of your work if you do so.

Illus. 91. Made by Arlette Testan- ière, this wall hanging measures about 19 inches by 19 inches (.51 metres by .51 metres).

Illus. 92. Made by Marcel Chik- hanovitch, this wall hanging meas- ures about 45 inches by 55 inches (1.15 metres by 1.40 metres).

A Few Wall Hangings

Here are some beautiful examples of patchwork, which should inspire you to make imaginative creations of your own. The next chapter discusses various ways to hang up your completed patchworks.

Illus. 91. Here, the visible stitches outline and enhance certain elements of the com- position. The bright border is especially striking in contrast to the rest of the picture.

Illus. 92. This charming picture has a uni- form quality throughout, which results as much from the primitive design as it does from the visible stitches.

Illus. 93. Here again, the patchwork appliqués are sewn with deliberately visible fine embroidery stitches. The alternating same color stitching and contrasting color stitching underline the importance of this embroidery in creating the total effect.

Illus. 94. In this photo, you see the effect of different patches appliquéd with a sewing- machine zig-zag stitch. This method does not really detract from the charm of the work; however, it's not the most classic way of sewing this time-honored craft.

Illus. 95. The stitches of this picture are quite visible, resulting in a charming sim- plicity that is unique.

Illus. 93. Made by Evelyne Cholvy, this wall hanging measures about 21 inches by 16 inches (.56 metres by .40 metres).

Illus. 94. Made by Yvette Termikelian, this wall hanging measures about 28 inches by 15 inches (.70 metres by .37 metres).

Illus. 95. Made by Germaine Barthélémy, this wall hanging measures about 58 inches by 43 inches (1.48 metres by 1.10 metres).

Illus. 96. Slipping a piece of wooden dowelling through fabric strips made from the same material as the background of this village scene is an appropriate and attractive way to hang the piece. Andrée Loiselot made this simplistic rural hanging. It measures about 28 inches by 26 inches (.70 metres by .64 metres).

Hanging a Patchwork Picture

If you want to hang a patchwork picture, there are several ways to do it:

1. You can hang it by simply passing a long nail through a large colored bead and then nailing the patchwork to the wall.

2. You can sew some carpet binding or other strong material to the upper edge of the front and back of the picture. Sew rings to this band at regular intervals—every 4 inches (10 cm.) or so. Then hammer some nails into the wall at the same intervals.

3. You can attach a piece of edging or strong ribbon to the back of the upper edge of your patchwork. Sew along both edges of the ribbon, but leave the corners open. This forms a kind of sleeve on the back of the patchwork, through which you insert a piece of bamboo or dowelling. This not only gives an even tension to the patchwork, but is a neat, invisible hanger.

4. You can also make hanging straps or loops from the same fabric as the patchwork's background, as you can see in Illus. 96, or from a different, contrasting fabric, or from a solid-colored material which harmonizes with your patchwork. By slipping a piece of dowelling or a bamboo rod through these rings, you ensure an even tension and wrinkle-free appearance for your creation. For this technique, you do need to add some sort of reinforcement along the top of the patchwork, between the background piece and an added backing.

Illus. 97. A brilliant sun, lush greenery, and a charming country home—all made by knitting! As you can see, you can even use scraps of knitting yarn to create unique patchwork projects. Josette Mostephaoui made this one, which measures about 34 inches by 21 inches (.83 metres by .56 metres).

Illus. 98. This is only half of a striking and colorful knitted patchwork bedspread made by Colette Dupont. The entire piece measures about 60 inches by 94 inches (1.55 metres by 2.40 metres).

Opposite page:
Illus. 99. Bright colors outstandingly bordered in black characterize this woollen, crocheted bedspread. Crocheted squares are a popular and fun-to-make component of patchwork creations. Nicole Clarence made this country bedspread.

Knitted Patchwork

Assembling blocks made of knitted patterns can result in marvelous patchworks. Knitting patches is advantageous because you can create an infinite number of designs in a rainbow of colors. It also allows you to construct the large, complex surfaces needed for afghans and wall hangings without having whole, heavy projects hanging from your needles—using small scraps of wool! You can easily take the blocks with you to work or wherever you go.

To plan your knitted blocks, you can use any designs intended for cross-stitch embroidery, because both techniques use the same grid layout to graph their patterns. You must knit one stitch for each square on the embroidery grid. You can also transpose the sketches found throughout the pages of this book.

If you use the same basic colors in all the blocks of the patchwork, you will highlight the central patterns, just as in crocheted patchworks (see page 97). But, you can also choose to make monochromatic blocks with fine results. For instance, if you combine various tones of beige and natural earth shades, you can make a lovely, subtly-colored bedspread for a modern bedroom.

You can assemble the different sections of a knitted patchwork into a wall hanging without necessarily putting the blocks into a geometric composition. You can make them into imaginative pictures, such as the landscape in Illus. 97, which is made of patches of different sizes and colors, just like fabric.

To make a patchwork like this, you need to make two full-sized sketches of the project first. Then, after you have chosen the colors you want to use, cut out each distinct area from one of the sketches. Knit that portion following the exact outline of the template.

Lay each knitted section in position on the second sketch to make sure the shapes match perfectly. Place the layout on your ironing board and carefully damp-iron. Pin each piece in place so that the outline of each matches the outline of its adjoining patch exactly. The elasticity of the knitting makes this an easy step.

Sew the pieces together with whip stitches on the underside of the knitting, adding a few stitches at stress points of the completed picture. Then, attach the whole creation to a fairly heavy backing material which will help it keep its shape.

If you are making a knitted patchwork bedspread, the backing not only hides the loose ends of yarn and the knots on the underside of the knitted work, but it prevents the work from unravelling when someone sits on the bed.

You can reinforce the backing of a knitted bedspread by knotting it, as described in the chapter *Quilting and Knotting* on page 79.

96

Crocheted Patchwork

Crocheted patchwork has been a popular member of the patchwork family for many years. For many people, the words "crocheted patchwork afghan" bring to mind a project consisting of hundreds of simple forms—usually squares—that are crocheted from scraps of yarn without any specific pattern in mind. The squares are assembled either without any specific order, or in such a way that the rows of crochet create a definite pattern from the dominant colors of the squares.

Car blankets, beach bags, shawls and other articles of clothing (sleeveless vests, jackets, skirts, scarves, for instance), as well as countless afghans and baby blankets are easy to make with this crochet technique which uses different sized and patterned squares. If you know how to crochet, you already know that there are countless varieties of squares you can make. Following are three simple patterns to choose from.

Opposite page:
Illus. 100. Subdued colors blend beautifully in this completely crocheted country landscape by Jeanne Korn. The creation measures about 47 inches by 41 inches (1.42 metres by 1.04 metres).

"Granny Square"

The most common patch design, shown in Illus. 101, is often called the "Granny Square."

Here's how you make it: Chain 4 stitches and close them in a circle with a slip stitch. Into this circle, make 12 double crochets.

2nd row: Make 6 doubles every 3 stitches (starting between the third and fourth stitches of the first row). That is, skip 3 stitches before inserting the crochet hook in between 2 stitches of the previous row to make 6 doubles. Do this 4 times altogether.

3rd row: Make 6 doubles at the center of each 6-stitch design of the preceding row, and 3 doubles between each of these designs.

Illus. 101. The most common crocheted patch design, the "Granny Square."

Note: Crochet terms and instructions given in this book are American. Substitute English terms as follows:

American	English
yarn over (yo)	wool round hook
chain (ch)	chain
slip stitch (sl st)	single crochet
single crochet (sc)	double crochet
half double crochet (hdc)	half treble crochet
double crochet (dc)	treble crochet

4th row: In the same way, make 6 doubles in the center of each 6-stitch motif of the preceding row and 3 doubles between each design.

5th row: All around the square, make a series of 3 doubles between each motif of the preceding row, but make 6 doubles at each corner (in the center of the 6-stitch motif of the preceding row) instead of the 3 doubles between 2 motifs in the preceding row.

6th row: Make 1 double between each double of the preceding row, making 3 doubles at each corner in the center of the 6-stitch corner of the preceding row.

You can make such squares all one color

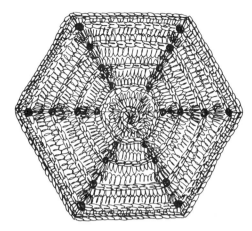

Illus. 102. This is the crocheted hexagon pattern described below.

or you can change the colors every row. When you have made enough squares for an entire project—whatever it is you choose —you can join the squares together, side by side, with single crochet stitches between the double crochets of each square.

Crocheted Hexagon

Here's how to make a crocheted hexagon like the one shown in Illus. 102.

Chain 7 stitches. Make 12 single crochet stitches into the first 6 chain stitches (2 in each), starting in the second chain from the hook. Close the circle with a single crochet stitch in the last chain stitch.

*Make 1 single crochet stitch in the next stitch and then 3 single crochet stitches into the second single crochet stitch from the preceding row. Repeat 5 times from *.

Finish the circle with a slip stitch. Make 1 single crochet stitch in the next stitch and then 3 single crochet stitches in the second stitch of the first 3 single crochet stitches from the previous row. Skip 1 single crochet stitch and do 1 single crochet stitch in the next stitch after that. Do 3 single crochet stitches in the second stitch of the next 3 single crochet group from the previous row. Continue this way until the hexagon is as large as you want.

To join your hexagons to complete your project, sew the backs together with whip stitches using the same wool with which you crocheted.

Illus. 103. If you follow the instructions for the pop-corned square described on this page and the next, your finished design should look like this.

Popcorned Square

Illus. 103 shows a square with crocheted "popcorns" whose color contrasts with the background. In creating a project using many of these squares, you can either make each one a different color, or you can alternate two colors within each square, thus creating an attractive pattern.

To begin, chain a row of 13 stitches and close the circle with a slip stitch.

1st circle: Make 1 single crochet stitch in the 1st of the 13 chain stitches, then 5 chain stitches, 1 single crochet stitch in the 4th chain stitch, 5 chain stitches, 1 single crochet stitch in the 7th chain stitch, 5 chain stitches, 1 single crochet stitch in the 10th chain stitch, 5 chain stitches, and 1 single crochet stitch in the 13th chain stitch.

2nd circle: *Make 1 single crochet stitch in the 1st single crochet stitch of the 1st circle. Then make 1 single crochet stitch in the 1st of the 5 chain stitches; then 5 chain stitches, then 1 single crochet stitch in the 5th chain stitch. Repeat 3 times from *. The third time, end the row with the 5 chain stitches.

3rd circle: Make 5 single crochet stitches

in the 3 single crochet stitches underneath and in the chain stitches that directly precede and follow these single crochet stitches. Then make 5 chain stitches, 5 single crochet stitches, and so on, all around.

4th circle: Continue to increase as in the 3rd circle but also make the 1st "popcorn" (make 4 double crochets in the same stitch, place the crochet hook from behind into the first double crochet and make a single crochet stitch) after 3 single crochet stitches in each triangle of the square (that is, into the middle single crochet stitch in the triangle). If the popcorn appears on the back side of your work, simply push it through to the right side with your finger.

In the following rows, you continue to add the popcorn stitches in every 2nd row every 3 single crochet stitches, until the square is the size you want. See Illus. 103 for an idea of how to lay out the popcorns.

If you want, the yarn for the popcorns can contrast with the background color. If so,

you should cut it every time you finish a group of popcorns. Simply fold and tuck the beginning and end of each color of yarn into the surrounding stitches.

You can assemble these squares as you would an afghan made of hexagonal patches, using whip stitches on the back side. Or, you can surround each square with a crocheted border the same color as the popcorns, and then whip stitch the squares together with this same wool.

For a pretty finish, you can trim the outside border of the afghan after joining all the patches together by crocheting a band in whatever width you want. You can use one or many colors, depending on the effect you want. If you make the popcorns in many colors, you can make the border from different lengths of these same colors, separating them with sections of the dominant or background colors. Don't forget to add extra stitches in each row to form the corners.

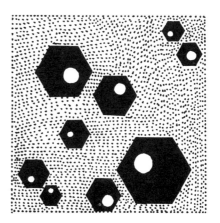

Ideas for Patchwork Designs

  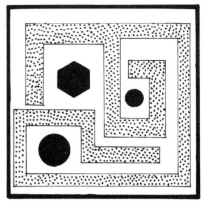

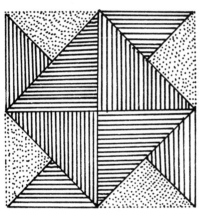  

  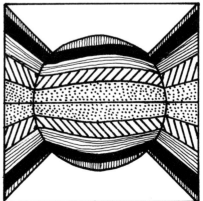

Illus. 104.

Illus. 105. From top to bottom and from left to right, these traditional quilt patterns are: "Tulip Crib," "Oak Leaf," "Tulip Design," "Prairie Flower," "Lobster," "Bridal Wreath," "The Rose of Sharon," "The Melon," "Hearts and Flowers."

Illus. 106. From top to bottom and from left to right, these traditional quilt patterns are: "Stepping Stones," "Crazy Ann," "Star of Bethlehem," "Starlight," "Old Tippecanoe," "Free Trade Patch," "Formosa Tea Leaf," "Sunflower" or "Blazing Sun" or "Blazing Star," "Triple Sunflower."

Illus. 107. This classic geometric pattern can be artfully constructed using contrasting colors of ribbons or cloth strips.

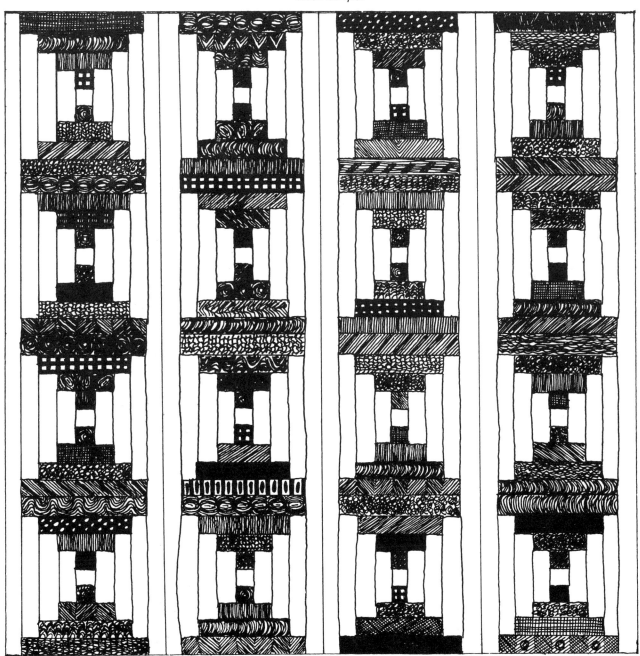

Illus. 108. Simple yet diverse, this motif is called "The Old Woman's Road."

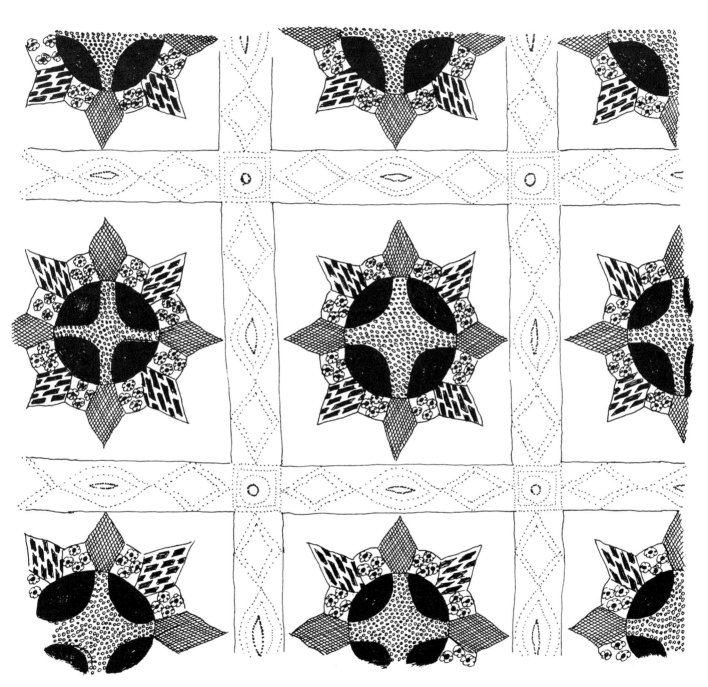

Illus. 109. The design pictured here is entitled "Caesar's Crowns."

Illus. 110. This sketch of the classic "Log Cabin" pattern shows the impression of depth that you can achieve by using different intensities of colors around the central squares.

Illus. 111. This is another sketch of the "Log Cabin" pattern shown on the previous page. Notice that even though the patches have the same shape as those in Illus. 110, using different colors and patterns can drastically alter the effect of the composition.

Illus. 112. From top to bottom and from left to right, these traditional quilt patterns are: "Pine Tree," "Temperance Tree," "Forbidden-Fruit Tree," "Poinsettia" or "Flower of Christmas," "Wild Rose," "Pomegranate," "Bird of Paradise," "Square and Circle," "Hollyhock Wreath."

Illus. 113. You can experiment with a single motif, simply altering its outlines, as was done here with a basic yet stylized star design.

Index